DIRTY DAVE
DOES #2

by the same author
Dirty Dave's 101 X-Rated Jokes

DIRTY DAVE DOES #2
101 MORE X-RATED JOKES
Illustrated by Peter Bramley

BELL PUBLISHING COMPANY
NEW YORK

This 1984 edition is published by Bell Publishing Company, One Park Avenue, New York, New York 10016

Manufactured in the United States of America

Library of Congress Cataloging in Publication Data

Main entry under title:
Dirty Dave does #2.
   1. Sex—Anecdotes, facetiae, satire, etc.
I. Bramley, Peter. II. Title: Dirty Dave does number two.
PN6231.S54D57 1984   818′.5402   83-21425
ISBN: 0-517-429500
h g f e d c b a

CONTENTS

PREFACE

Welcome back to the land of erotic make-believe, peopled with raunchy ladies, horny men, and sexual objects, subjects, and rejects. In *Jokes and the Unconscious* Freud said, "Only when we rise to a society of a more refined education do the formal conditions for jokes play a part. . . . It cannot be doubted that the desire to see what is sexually exposed is the original motive of smut." André Gide, the famous French author, referring to dirty jokes, wrote, "They remain anonymous and form part of a kind of folklore where the genius of a race emerges."

In light of the above statements, "back by popular demand" is a most satisfying introduction to *Dirty Dave Does #2*. If you've read *Dirty Dave's 101 X-Rated Jokes* and/or are about to read *Dirty Dave Does #2*, take heart in the thought that you are part of "a society of a more refined education," and that you are helping to perpetuate "a kind of folklore where the genius of a race emerges."

Now that we've established that it's perfectly okay to enjoy a good dirty joke without the aid of a flashlight under the bed covers at night, we can appreciate Freud when he says the uttering of an undisguised indecency "gives the first person enjoyment and makes the third person laugh."

And laughter is what it's all about! If Dirty Dave makes you laugh, then we enjoy success. If you laugh you'll probably have better digestion and certainly a less tense libido. So enter Dirty Dave's world of erotic misbehavior with a healthy appetite and a clear conscience. And remember, share it with a friend!

Dirty Dave

New York City
1984

DIRTY DAVE
DOES # 2

Banana Split

"Listen, you little bushwhacker," said the irate mother to her diminutive cowboy son, "I've got to get a present for your sister's birthday, and how can I shop if you're all over the place?"

"Bang bang!" said little Nathan, unholstering his matching cap-pistol forty-fives and blasting her brains all over toyland.

"That does it! I told you not to point those things at me. Now get over there to that soda fountain and stay put. Give him anything he wants, but keep him here," she said to the buxom woman behind the counter.

"Hi there, partner. What'll you have?"

"Banana split," answered little Nathan.

"You want three scoops of ice cream?"

"Yeah!"

"You want two bananas?"

"Yeah!"

"You want three kinds of syrup?"

"Yeah!"

"You want whipped cream on top?"

"Yeah!"

"You want nuts on it?"

"Yeah!"

"You want your nuts crushed?"

"No! You want your tits shot off?" replied the minute cowboy, drawing his shootin' irons.

Cutbacks

Lord Beaverbottom arrived home at his country estate after a brutal week of losses in the millions on the stock exchange. It was indeed a black Friday for the Beaverbottom empire.

The first thing he did upon arriving home was to inquire after the whereabouts of Lady Beaverbottom. He was told she was having her tarot cards read and couldn't be disturbed, but disturb her he did.

"Oh really, Reggie, you are such a bore," said Lady Beaverbottom when he burst into the solarium. "I distinctly left instructions I was not to be disturbed while Dr. Whacko was reading my cards."

"Hit the road, Dr. Whacko!" ordered Lord Beaverbottom.

"Reggie!"

"I said hit the road, Whacko, before I smear your greasy little ass all over the philodendra!"

When Dr. Whacko had beat a hasty retreat, Lord Beaverbottom said, "I'll put it to you straight, Charlotte. We're very nearly wiped out. The Beaverbottom empire has bottomed out, as it were. We'll have to sell the house in Barbados, the villa in Majorca as well, and we'll have to get rid of at least two of the cars. I can probably scrape enough together to keep us on here, but we'll have to let most of the servants go, including the cook. You'll just have to learn how to cook."

"I've got an idea, Reggie," replied Lady Beaverbottom. "Why not fire the gardener instead, and *you* can learn how to fuck!"

Action

Karl walked into the Pink Pillow Motel and said to the desk clerk, "Hey, buddy, I'm a salesman from out of town, and Big Jack told me to come here and mention his name if I wanted some real hot action."

"Oh, yeah? Any friend of Big Jack is a potential deadbeat. What kind of action you lookin' for?"

"The hotter the better. I know every position and every technique to drive the little girls wild. I can get my rocks off in fourteen languages. Spent some time in the army, ya know."

"Whoopee. Well, I suppose you're all right. Run on down there to cabin twelve. Tell Rhonda to give you the works. You need anything, just ring the desk. What's your pleasure? I'll send a bottle along."

"Wild Turkey," answered Karl with a gale of laughter. "Get it? Wild Turkey? I'm a gobblin' fool!"

"Well, you're half right. By the way, Rhonda has a black belt, so nothing kinky."

After Karl's action with Rhonda, he went back to the desk clerk to settle his bill.

"Nothing doing, buddy, this one's on the house," said the desk clerk. "Rhonda just phoned in you're one superdicked salesman and the best walking advertisement we could have. Now get out of here, you gobblin' fool, and don't do anything I wouldn't do. Gobble, gobble!"

The next night Karl went back, swaggered up to the desk clerk, and said, "Tell Redhot Rhonda that Krazy Karl's back!"

"That'll be fifty bucks out front. You got thirty minutes, so don't blow it!"

"Hey, buddy, this is your old pal Karl. What's this fifty bucks out front shit? Last night I was king of the hill!"

"Yeah, but we're not filming tonight!"

Shipwreck

What started out to be a pleasant afternoon outing turned into disaster when a squall suddenly blew up out of nowhere and capsized the small pleasure boat. Only Ned and Jed and Dusty managed to swim to the tiny, deserted island and safety.

After the first month, Dusty was so disgusted with what she was allowing Ned and Jed to do to her, she killed herself.

After the second month, Ned and Jed were so disgusted with what they were still doing to her, they buried her.

After the third month, Ned and Jed were so disgusted with what they were doing to each other, they dug her up again!

The Great Divide

What a honeymoon! It was already the fourth day and Bob and Susan hadn't left the room. They were living on love and take-out Chinese. Waiting until they were married to make love had been a real trial, but they were glad they had and were making up for those months of frustration. They'd made love in every position and every conceivable combination and their passion hadn't cooled a bit.

"Oh, baby girl," said Bob from atop her, "can you spread your legs a little wider?"

"Oh, Bobby," panted Susan, "like this?"

"Oh yes, baby girl, spread them a little wider," begged Bob.

"Like this?" gasped Susan.

"Oh yes, Susan," sweated Bob, "a little wider."

"Oh, Bobby," heaved Susan, "are you trying to get your balls inside?"

"No, baby girl," answered Bob. "I'm trying to get them out!"

Ah, 'Tis a Sad Day

"Father, might I ask you a wee bit of a favor?"

"Certainly, darling girl. On this sad day of Paddy O'Reilly's wake, his dearly beloved can surely ask a wee bit of a favor. What might it be?"

"Get me his penis."

Father O'Malley took two steps back and said three fast Hail Marys. But she would not be dissuaded, and, fearing for her sanity, he managed with some embarrassment to get her husband's penis for her.

Late that evening as Rosie O'Reilly sat in her

kitchen thinking sad thoughts about the wake and eternity, her sister peeped in.

"Hmmm, what's that sweet smell of cooking? What've you got simmering in that saucepan on the stove?"

"Paddy's penis," answered Rosie, her eyes clear of sadness and deep with content.

Rosie's sister froze, her face distorted with the G-force of shock. Rosie smiled benignly and said, "For years I ate it his way. Now I'm having it mine!"

General Store

"Honey, on your way home from school today, stop off at the general store and pick me up a pound of peas. Now run along or you'll miss the school bus. And don't forget to ask Mr. Wade how his wife is doing," she called after her son Freddy, who slammed the screen door, jumped off the porch, and shot the guts out the asshole of an aged hen laying her eggs in a clump of irises next to the steps when he landed on her.

"Mom! Let's have chicken for supper!" he called back to his mother as he ran down the road to catch the school bus.

After school he raced into the general store, slamming the screen door behind him, and was trying to rifle the gumball machine when Mr. Wade asked, "And what can I do for you today, young man?"

"My mom wants a pound of peas, and how's your wife?"

Referring to the peas, Mr. Wade said, "Split or whole?"

And Freddy said, "She did?!"

Measure for Measure

The SS gruppenführer looked over the ragtail group of captured resistance fighters. Having a fanciful eye for a proud buttock or a well-packed trouser front, he selected three of the captives to step out of line. The others were taken out and shot.

"Ach, meine kleine naughty, naughty boys," chided the SS gruppenführer. "Why should you be so bad as to cause nasties for the glorious Reich mit your little bombs und leaflets. Such pretty ones as you should be enjoying your youth. So, if among you, you can show me eighteen inches of pricken, I will let you go free. Now drop your pants so I can measure."

They did, and he pulled out a ruler, taking his time and making sure to get full measure. The first lad measured in at nine throbbing inches, which pleased the SS gruppenführer very much. And he was not displeased when the second lad measured in at eight inches. He barely glanced at the inch-and-a-half mark on the ruler for the third lad.

"Such a shame, just another pretty face. However, I will keep my word und release you, but if I ever see your faces again, you will be shot on the spot!"

Later the three lads were drinking some wine in celebration of their narrow escape when the first lad said, "How lucky you two are that I was with you with my nine inches."

The second lad said, "Oui, and how lucky you are that I had my eight inches."

The third lad said, "Oui, and how lucky you both are, mes amis, that I could get mine hard!"

Riddled

When Wyeth was a struggling, out-of-work young actor, he was invited to a soiree at a famous film producer's home. The film producer's wife was an avid riddle fanatic, and riddles were the game of the day. When it was Wyeth's turn he asked, "What's round, hot and moist, and covered with hair?"

When everyone had given up in horror, he said simply, "It's a cunt."

"Get this man's coat, Blair!" ordered the outraged film producer's wife, and Wyeth was banished from the cream of film society.

Years later after Wyeth had become a respected and very successful stage and film star, he was again invited to the same home. And again riddles were the game of the hour.

When it was Wyeth's turn he asked, "What's round, hot and moist, and covered with hair?"

The glittering assemblange all beamed at him in happy anticipation of his brilliant answer.

"My hat and coat, Blair," said Wyeth. "It's still a cunt!"

Big-Game Hunter

Dr. Itch, the dermatologist, was an all-around sportsman who enjoyed the savagery of the hunt as well as the subtlety of golf. His office walls were lined with golf trophies and the stuffed heads of the moose, deer, and antelope he'd shot. On his desk were a pair of bronzed golf balls.

His new receptionist, Miss Perfect, commented on

his trophies and animal heads and asked, "Gee, Dr. Itch, what're those bronzed balls on your desk?"

"Oh, they're golf balls, Miss Perfect," replied Dr. Itch as he applied poison-ivy lotion to her buttocks.

Several days later during a break between patients, Miss Perfect went into Dr. Itch's office to have some watermelon lotion applied to her melons and noticed two ordinary white golf balls in the ashtray on his desk.

"Oh, you shot another golf," said Miss Perfect. "You going to bronze his balls, too?"

Snow White

"Listen, Mr. Swaggart, this is Mary Bullblower's father, and I want to know what you're going to do about your son!"

"Calm down, Mr. Bullblower. What seems to be the problem?"

"The problem? The problem is your son peed in the snow on our front lawn!"

"Ah yes, that sounds like one of his stunts. Have no fear, Mr. Bullblower, I'll speak to him, and please accept my apologies. He's not a bad boy—"

"Hold on there, Swaggart, that's not all!"

"Oh? What else, Mr. Bullblower?"

"When your son peed in the snow, he spelled out my daughter's name, that's what else!"

"I understand they're going through a teenage case of puppy love. I'm really sorry if he caused you any embarrassment."

"Embarrassment, my ass! It was in her handwriting!"

Grandpa Sloane

Grandpa Sloane turned up at Madame Helene's place a little after midnight with a real snootful and raring to go.

"I want the broad with the biggest pair of tits and the tightest pussy you got!" yelled the drunk old man as he slipped on the Persian carpet and pitched into the potted fern. Madame Helene didn't like old men, and drunk old men turned her piggy little eyes into darts of flame.

"Shut your trap, you old fool, and get the fuck out of my fern!" screamed the madam.

"Fern, shmern, bring on the biggest pair of tits and tightest pussy you got! I'm a spendin' man!"

"All right, fool, you've had it!" roared Madame Helene.

"Oh, I have, have I!" giggled Grandpa Sloane. "Well, in that case, how much do I owe you?!"

Born in a Trunk

"Doctor, this is a little embarrassing, but I don't think my penis is of normal size. I mean, it's so small."

After the examination the doctor agreed, somewhat too emphatically, it was indeed the smallest penis he'd ever seen. However, he assured the young man he could increase the size of his penis and extracted a length of gray, rubbery tubing from a rundown glass case.

"Now, young man, don't think this is some witch doctor's remedy from darkest Africa, because even if it is, I know it works. Slip this piece of elephant's trunk over the little fellow, tie it tightly, and leave it in place for two weeks. Don't even take it off when you shower. It must remain in place for two weeks, and I guarantee you'll have a wanger any man would envy."

After the two-week period, the young man removed the elephant's trunk from his penis and was thrilled with the results. He couldn't wait to make a date with that lovely little redhead down the hall at work now that he had an instrument he was sure would tickle her fancy all the way up to her eyeballs. He escorted her to a chic, white-linen-tablecloth, candlelit restaurant. While they were reading the menu, he felt an odd sensation from his lap, and to his great surprise, over the edge of the table crept his penis, sniffing its blind way to the basket of dinner rolls. It sucked one to itself and slipped silently back out of sight under the table. He was so fascinated with this performance he didn't notice that his date was also watching.

"Wow!" she said with great admiration. "Can you do that again!"

"Well, yes, I think I can, but I'm not sure I could take another hard roll stuffed up my ass!"

Four on the Wing

The patrolman hauled the four rowdies up to the desk sergeant.

"All right, fellows, quiet down. I know, police brutality, you've got your rights—now shut up! You, with the pink hair, what's your name and occupation?"

"My name's McCoy," replied the pink-haired rowdy, "and I'm a cork soaker."

"Very funny, wise guy. I didn't ask about your sex life. What's your occupation?"

"No, I really am a cork soaker. I work for the winery on Canal Street."

"And you?" asked the sergeant. "What's your name and occupation?"

"My name's McCoy, and I'm a coke sacker."

"Everyone's a comedian these days. Now, I'm being a nice guy with you fruit loops, so come on, huh?"

"But, Sergeant, my name *is* McCoy, and I'm a coke sacker for the Cherry Charcoal Company on Fleet Street."

The sergeant sighed with infinite patience and said to the third, "Name and occupation."

"My name's McCoy, and I'm a sock tucker."

"Right," said the sergeant, resigned to frustration. "And you? I suppose your name's McCoy, too?"

"That's right, Sergeant," said the fourth with a wink, "but I'm the *real* McCoy!"

Half-Baked

Bart and Chip had a great day at the beach. Well, at least Bart did. Gorgeous gal after gorgeous gal found her way to their blanket, but all chatted up Bart and ignored poor old Chip. Bart took several long strolls in the dunes with their secret spots for loving, each stroll with a different knockout piece. Chip held down the blanket and guarded the valuables.

Back in their motel room that night, Chip said, "I'm going home. This vacation sucks. You're a turd!"

Bart said, "Yes. No. And no. What's your problem?"

"You get all the girls," whined Chip.

"You know why? Because I'm smart."

"You suck moose cock, that's why," said Chip and started packing.

"I'll ignore that. Hey, listen, don't be a jerk. Do what I do, and you too can have fun, fun, fun. Put a baked potato in your swim trunks—the doxies'll notice you then."

"Yeah?"

So the next day at the beach Chip slipped a baked potato into his trunks. But the day went just as the one before.

That evening Chip said, "Well, big help you are. Fun, fun, fun, bullshit! You still got all the girls, and all I got was sand fleas!"

"Can I make a suggestion?" asked Bart.

"No!"

"Tomorrow try the baked potato in the *front* of your trunks."

The Ex

"Hey, Ron, isn't that your ex-wife, Cindy, at that table over in the corner?"

"The bitch."

"Can you see who she's with? That potted palm's blocking him."

"I don't care who she's with."

"Still smitten, eh?"

"Smitten, shitten. She's a bitch. I hope she's with Jack the Ripper—only he hasn't got a prayer."

"I admire your control, I'd be as curious as hell. Oh, he just leaned out. Looks like Max."

"Max?!"

"Hey, Ron, where're you going?"

Ron weaved his way through the tables to the other side of the restaurant, his stomach churning acid, and said, "Hello, Max. Hello, Cindy. How's that old, tired pussy of yours?"

Smiling, she gave him her best deb look and said, "Oh, just fine . . . once you get past the tiny bit that's been used!"

Remember Last Summer?

Little Joey hated closed doors, particularly when he was too small to reach up, turn the knob, and open them. But now that he was tall enough to reach the knob, a closed door meant nothing to him. That's how he happened to catch his mother naked in the bathroom.

His little eyes widened at what he saw. He pointed to the patch of curling blond hair between her legs and said, "I don't have that, Mommy. What is it?"

Joey's mother was no prude, but caught so totally unprepared, she offered a faltering explanation. "Do you remember last summer when Daddy was chopping all that firewood?"

"Yes," answered Joey.

"And do you remember how I got so sick last summer?"

"Yes."

"Well, that's where your daddy accidentally hit me with the axe and why I was so sick."

"Gee, that's too bad," sympathized little Joey. "Got you right in the cunt, didn't he?!"

On the Hill

"In recognition of your fifty years' service as lavatory attendant in the Senate Building, I'd now like to present you with this genuine, simulated-gold-plated pocket watch," intoned the pompous senator from the South. "During your fifty years here on the Hill, you must have seen some impressive changes in our fair capital."

"Well, yes, sir, I have. But beggin' your pardon, sir, it's not so much the city has changed but the people. Why, in the old days they were gentlemen to a man. But now? Let me give you an example. Yesterday I had a senator in one booth, buggering his page. In another booth a senator was mixing that free-base cocaine snortin' stuff. And in the next booth a senator was looking at one of those trashy girlie magazines and floggin' his hog to beat the band.

"With all that perversion going on, in the last booth another senator was taking a good old-fashioned shit. Let me tell you, sir, it was like a breath of fresh air!"

Ship of the Desert

"Okay, Akmed, I'll take the damn camel. I've checked every camel dealer in town, and no one else has a camel that'll make the distance."

"Five hundred miles is nothing for my sweet Sultan, the swiftest and surest of all camels. Just remember what I told you. If he stops after you get out in the desert, all he wants is for you to jack him off, and he'll fly like the wind!"

"That's all he wants, is it?" said J. P. as he mounted the smelly beast and doggedly set out on his journey. Seventy-five miles into the desert, Sultan stopped dead in his tracks and refused to budge.

J. P. crossed himself and said, "God help me," climbed down, and ran around to the camel's nose. He wrapped his hand around an imaginary camel cock and slid it up and down, up and down. Sultan pulled back his lips into a camel grin and nodded up and down, up and down. So J. P. masturbated him and climbed aboard, and off they went. Another hundred miles into the desert, Sultan again slammed on his brakes and screeched to a halt.

"You must be joking!" said J. P. But he wasn't. When J. P. jerked his hand up and down under the camel's nose, Sultan grinned and nodded in smug consent. So J. P. masturbated him again.

When they were a hundred and fifty miles into the desert, isolated beyond any rescue, the camel dug his heels in the sand and wouldn't move.

"Great horny bastard!" said J. P. He jumped off, ran in front of the camel, and jerked his hand up and down. Sultan looked down his hairy, bulbous nose, shook his head firmly from side to side, then formed his camel lips into a big round *O*, and pushed his head forward and back, forward and back.

Sticks and Stones

"Why so glum, chum?" asked Dandy Dan.

"Nobody likes me," answered Slim Jim.

"Oh, come on, everybody likes you."

"How come I can't get laid then?"

"Oh. *That* kind of likes you."

"It's 'cause of my wooden eye, you know. It turns the ladies against me 'cause they think I'm creepy with my wooden eye."

"Hmmm. Well, what about Sweet Sally over there? Why not ask her?"

"Sweet Sally, the hunchback?"

"Tut, tut, tut. She's got a lovely face—well, passable —and she's awful sweet. And besides, maybe she wouldn't mind your wooden eye. Did you ever think of that? Give it a whirl!"

Slim Jim ambled over to where Sweet Sally sat hunched over a table by herself.

"Mind if I sit down?"

"Please do, Slim Jim," said Sweet Sally in her sweetest voice.

"You've got a real sweet voice, Sweet Sally. Would you like me to fuck you?"

"Oh, would I! Would I!" she cried wildly.

"Hunchback! Hunchback!" he shouted back at her and stomped out of the saloon.

Out to Lunch

Frankie, Larry, and Phil were having hot dogs and beer for lunch on the observation deck at the top of the Empire State Building in New York City.

"Let's hear it for the greatest city in the world!" cheered Frankie.

"The greatest titty!" chimed in Larry.

"The biggest clitty!" said Phil.

"Mouse hang, what do you know about clitties?" jeered Frankie.

"Audrey said you have a dirty wiener," accused Larry.

"Yeah, well Audrey shouldn't talk with her mouth full," answered Phil.

"One small mouthful for Audrey, one giant experience for Phil," said Frankie.

"What's all this *small* shit? If I tossed my dick over the edge here, it'd break windows all the way down to the sixty-third floor when it hit," claimed Phil.

"That's all, huh?" said Larry. "If I tossed mine over the edge, they'd think it was midnight at nigh noon all the way down to the bank!"

"Stand back, midget meat," said Frankie and went through an elaborate pantomime of unzipping his fly, unreeling his tool, and hoisting the great weight of it over the edge. After watching it descend for a while, he took several quick steps back, then to the left, then several quick steps to the right, then back, then forward.

"What're you doing, the cha-cha?" asked Larry.

"Just dodging traffic!" replied Frankie.

Roly-Poly

Three friends joined a health club on a two-for-one-plus-one-free seven-day trial membership, primarily because all the facilities except the showers and locker rooms were enjoyed by both men and women, and they wanted the opportunity to leer at the young ladies and make suggestive comments about them behind their backs.

These three musketeers had a grand old time pretty much making fools out of themselves playing at bench pressing and aerobics. Then they hit the showers to freshen up before going out on the town to really make assholes out of themselves.

One of them was pretty obese, and since they had no female victims at hand for their juvenile wit, the two who hadn't gone totally to fat were giving the tubby one a rough time.

"Be sure to wash your balls real good, Curly. They haven't seen the light of day for a long time. Must be real ripe down there."

"Yeah, Curly, when's the last time you saw your little pecker? You really ought to diet, ya know?"

"Dye it? Dye it?" panicked Curly. "Why? What color is it now?"

A Kick in the Teeth

"Morris," said Laura, "are you sorry we're having this blind date?"

Morris blushed and said, "No, it's not that."

"Then what is it? Have I done something to offend you?"

"No, of course you haven't. It's just . . . May I be honest with you?"

"Please do. I think you're a nice fellow and we could become friends, if at least we can talk to each other."

"I guess you've noticed I don't relate well to women. It's my mother's fault. She always told me never to get involved with women because they have teeth in their vaginas and would chew my penis off!" This last was said with great effort and a paroxysm of blushing.

Laura was stunned. After a few moments' thought, she said, "Morris, I'm amazed that your mother would lie to you like that, and if you're willing, I'd like to prove it to you. Don't think this is my style, but will you come to my apartment right now, never mind dinner, and let me show you she was lying?"

After some initial resistance, he agreed, and they went to Laura's apartment. She opened a bottle of wine, and after a few glasses, removed her clothes and invited him to inspect her vagina for teeth. He tentatively moved to her side, and on her assurance she would consider it just another gynecological examination, gingerly opened her vagina.

He gently felt around the labia minora, the clitoris, and deeper inside.

"See? What did I tell you? No teeth."

"Yeah, you're right," agreed Morris. "But your gums sure are in terrible shape!"

Bird of a Different Color

Poor Aunty Jill, thought the pet-shop owner. Why'd she have to go and buy that parrot with the saltiest language he'd ever heard? "Oh well, Pukey," he said to his tabby cat, "I warned her, but she never did listen to a good piece of advice."

Aunty Jill was well pleased with her brightly colored feathered little friend until he croaked at her, "Light me up a stogie, baby, and suck my ass to get the draft started!"

Aunty Jill stood there with her mouth hanging open, not believing her own ears. Then the parrot said, "Spit, sit, and spin on this, baby. You're really turning me on!"

Aunty Jill sprang into action. She grabbed the parrot from his cage, rushed to the kitchen, and hacked him to pieces with a carving knife.

She swept up the pieces, raced to the bathroom, and threw them into the commode. The door bell rang, and she ran to see what the postman had brought. The tea kettle whistled, and she ran to make a cup of tea. Then the chickens needed feeding. Later she forgetfully went to the bathroom to relieve herself. The parrot's one good eye looked up out of the bowl as she sat, and she heard him croak from beneath her, "I'll get well, baby, I'll get well. If you can live with a gash like that, I'll get well!"

Wind

"Good afternoon, Mr. Lang. What seems to be the problem?"

"Well, Doctor, lately I have this—"

"Good heavens," interrupted the doctor, "what's that terrible smell?"

"That's it, Doctor," said Mr. Lang dismally. "That's my problem. I don't know why, but lately I've had this excessive flatulence. I mean, well, you know . . . I fart all the time."

"Mr. Lang, I'm quite aware of what 'flatulence' means. You needn't get scatalogical. But how do you stand that smell?"

"I'm really very sorry. You don't know how embarrassing it can be."

"No descriptions, please. I'm not without imagination. Drop your pants, bend over, and spread your cheeks. Let's get to the bottom of this."

When Mr. Lang did as he was told, he emitted another of his flower-wilting zephyrs, and the doctor lunged for a six-foot wooden pole with a nasty hook on the end that was leaning against the wall.

"Jesus, Doctor," asked Mr. Lang fearfully, "what are you going to do with that?"

"Open the window, you silly ass!" replied the doctor.

How Now, Brown Cow?

Grandpa Sloane took his best cow, Corabelle, over to Sioux City to have her bred by a champion stud bull named The Duff. He paid a pretty penny for the service and was supervising the job himself to make sure no minor-league bull was giving sweet Corabelle a cheap-thrills quickie.

While Grandpa Sloane was overseeing the operation, The Duff's owner's daughter wandered up and stood beside the old man. The old codger's heart skipped a beat when he saw her standing there. She was that beautiful.

"Afternoon, missy," said Grandpa Sloane, tipping his hat and rolling his eyes eagerly over her body.

"Hiya, pops!" she answered. "Looks like The Duff's having himself some fun."

"You can sure say that again," said Grandpa Sloane, almost drooling over her pointy teats jutting through the cotton of her T-shirt. He stepped nearer to her and whispered, "Swear to God, sweetie, I'd sure like to be doin' what he's doin' right now."

"Go right ahead, hot stuff," she answered. "She's your cow!"

Yellow Bird

"My canary is moping around, won't sing, and hardly eats enough to keep a bird alive," said Mr. Warbler to the pet-shop owner. "I'd like to buy a female bird in hopes she'll raise his spirits."

When Mr. Warbler put the golden little female canary in his bird's cage, the bird took one look at her, raced to the water spout, and preened until all his feathers were perfectly in line. Then he hopped over to her, gave her the eye, and chirped, "Hello there, sweet thing, want to share some seed?"

"Don't touch me," she chirped, "just don't touch me!" And she fluttered to the other side of the cage.

"Well, don't that beat all," he chirped, dumbfounded. He flew to her side and chirped, "I don't know what your problem is, sweet little mama, but what do you think you're here for?"

"I don't know what I'm here for," she answered, "but you better not touch me. I've got twerpes. It's a canarial disease, and there's no tweetment!"

The Obscene Phone Call

"Hello?"

"Hello, little girl. Is your mommy at home?"

"No."

"Don't hang up, little girl! Little girl, don't hang up. Little girl?"

"Hello?"

"Hello, now don't hang up, honey. Your mommy's not home?"

"No."

"Do you have a big sister?"

"Yes."

"Ohhh good. Is she at home? Now don't hang up."

"No."

"Oh, she's not. How old are you, little girl?"

"Four."

"Oh, well. . . . Poopoo-caca! Poopoo-caca!"

The Drugstore

Big Tex McNutty was alone in the big city for the first time, and frankly, he was nearly out of his mind. He'd never seen so many absolutely gorgeous women, with their lovely long legs, their big breasts bouncing freely in their skimpy blouses, and their big-city ways. They all seemed to look at him like God had put them there just for him to screw. Being a good Christian boy, he was having an awful time adjusting to walking around with a hard-on all the time and not enough nerve to do anything about it. So he went into a drugstore in search of some remedy for constant erection.

When he approached the counter, Edna turned to him and said, "Yes, sir, what can I do for you?"

"Ah, ah, ah . . ." was all Big Tex managed to say.

"Yes?" asked Edna with a tender smile.

"Well, er, ah . . ." said Big Tex, blushing wildly.

"Oh," said Edna, glancing over the counter down at his bulging crotch, "do you want some condoms?"

"What? No! I mean . . . Is there a man here?"

"Sir," said Edna gently, "I understand you may want something personal and would prefer a man to wait on you. But there isn't a man in this store, and I'm perfectly capable of serving you. Trust me."

"Well, gee, you see . . ." stammered Big Tex. Then in a flurry of words he blurted out, "I've got this raging hard-on I can't get rid of. What can you give me for it?"

"Just one moment, sir," said Edna and went into the back room. She returned shortly and said, "I've just consulted my sister, Ellen, who makes up the prescriptions. The best we can give you is the store and two hundred dollars cash!"

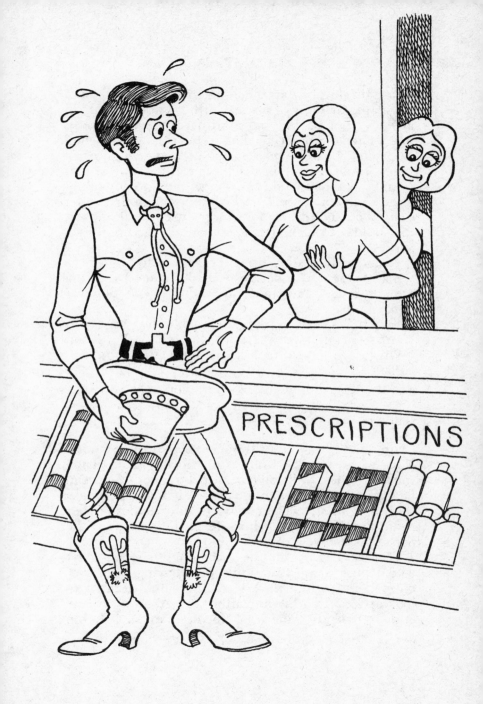

In the Navy

A certain naval captain had a strong aversion to the possibility that any of his seaworthy swabbies could in any way not be one-hundred-percent all-American male. Each sailor received an indoctrination kit when he came aboard which included a mimeographed sheet from the captain strictly forbidding any of that "namby-pamby, buddy-fucking, butt-stoking buggery!" Not being totally callous concerning the young sailors' needs, the captain didn't exclude, however, the standard five-finger, Rosie Palmer method of release.

One day after the ship had been out to sea several weeks, a crew member respectfully saluted the captain and said, "Captain, sir, there's been buggery aboard."

"What?" roared the captain in a blinding rage.

"Yes, sir, indeed there has," replied the sailor. "Why just this morning I tasted shit on the first mate's balls!"

She Saw the Light

Lynne had been one of the most beautiful and notorious whores in the history of whoring. But during the late sixties, while on a wild acid trip with a Korean hair merchant, she had a transcendental experience, saw the Christ, became reborn, and dedicated her beauty and the rest of her life to the service of the Salvation Army.

One of Lynne's cronies from her whoring days who'd missed most of the sixties (having been kidnapped into white slavery in Botswana) decided to look up her friend Lynne after her harrowing escape and return to America. Needless to say, Robin couldn't believe her ears when she was told of Lynne's conversion and went to an "experience" meeting Lynne was holding at the local chapter of the Army. Sure enough, there was the beautiful Lynne standing at the podium all dewy eyed and vestal-virginal, relating the experience of her conversion.

"Before I saw the light," said Lynne to her rapt, hushed audience, "it's true, I lay in the arms of many men. I've lain in the arms of husbands, fathers, soldiers, sailors, merchants, doctors, lawyers, pugilists, internists, hair dressers, tap dancers, and, yes, even taxicab drivers." She paused to allow the enormity of her past sins to penetrate. "But now that I have lain in the arms of Jesus—"

"That's right, kid," called Robin from the audience, "Fuck 'em. Fuck 'em all!"

Oh, Honey, Please

"Oh, honey, please. Just let me stick it in a little way."

"Johnny! I said no!"

"Oh, honey, please. I love you so much, and I'm so horny. Just let me rub the head against your panties."

"Yuck! Men are all pigs! All you want to do is fuck, fuck, fuck. I told you, no more freebies. You don't give a goat's gonads about me. All you care about is that damn dick of yours."

"Oh, honey, please. Let me cut the gash that never heals."

"That's disgusting! It's a vagina, and it's gonna cost you fifty bucks!"

"Fifty bucks?! You gotta be kidding."

"I'd rather sew it shut than do it for a penny less!"

"Well, a couple of stitches wouldn't hurt," mused Johnny.

Lady Godiva

A cabby driving along Park Avenue slammed on the brakes and came to a screeching halt when a naked woman jumped from between two parked cars into his way. She got in and said, "Eighteen-twelve Park Avenue, please, and I'm in a hurry!"

"Right, lady," the cabby responded and took off. After a couple of blocks, he began to wonder how she was going to pay. As the saying goes, she had no visible means of support. When they came to a red light, the cabby turned to the woman.

"Uh, lady, excuse me for asking, but how do you plan on paying the fare when we get there?"

She smiled coyly and pointed down between her legs.

He looked where she pointed and said, "Oh really? You got anything smaller?"

Harvard vs. Yale

The Harvard and Yale debating teams had ripped each other mercilessly all morning long, neither giving the other an edge in the finals of the debate competition. After the lunch break, it happened that the captains of both teams were at the men's room urinals at the same time.

The Harvard captain finished his business, zipped up, checked himself out in the mirror, and started to leave.

The Yale captain asked, "Don't they teach you to wash your hands after taking a piss at Harvard?"

The Harvard captain replied, "At Harvard, they teach us not to piss on our hands!"

Rubber-Dolly Folly

Captain Percival of the Royal Navy browsed through the novelty shop, not really shopping until the inflatable woman caught his eye. He beckoned the shopkeeper over and asked to what purpose the inflatable woman could be put.

"Come on, Captain, give it a little think through," said the shopkeeper. "Blow her up and have a bit of sport, eh?"

"You mean . . . ?"

"Indeed I do, sir. Anatomically correct, if you get my drift."

"You mean . . . ?"

"That's right, sir. All her orifices work. The pee-hole's even surrounded by genuine simulated hair. Very realistic, very realistic indeed, sir."

Captain Percival bought the latex lovely, smuggled her on board, and didn't give her another thought until several weeks out to sea when a severe gale blew up. Severe gales always stirred his passions, so he hot-footed it down to his cabin, inflated the rubber dolly, and was all set for a go-round when Midshipman Price called him topside.

Captain Percival threw a sheet over his rubber dolly, and bounded out. Midshipman Price glanced in, saw the female shape, doused the lights, screwed her silly, threw the sheet back over her, and dashed out. Moments later Captain Percival returned all afroth and ravaged her every orifice until nearly dawn.

Months later when his ship returned to port, Captain Percival hobbled painfully into the novelty shop and hurled the wadded up rubber dolly into the shopkeeper's face.

"What's the matter, sir, wasn't she realistic enough for you?" whined the shopkeeper.

"Indeed she was, you swine. The dirty slut gave me the clap!"

Hot Fudge Sundae

"Alfie, you're never going to believe what happened to me last night."

"What happened?"

"This whore took me to her room for a hot fudge sundae."

"Ice cream?"

"Wait till you hear this. She made me strip naked and lie spread-eagled on the bed."

"Yeah?"

"Then she packed vanilla ice cream all around my dick and balls, and then she poured hot fudge all over my dick."

"No!"

"Yes! Then she put whipped cream on the hot fudge and a cherry on top of that."

"What'd she do then?"

"Nothin'! It looked so good, I ate it myself!"

Quack, Quack!

The elderly lady went into the meat-and-poultry store and asked the young man behind the counter, "The sign outside says you got Long Island ducklings. You got?"

"Sure, lady, we got the best in town," answered the young man.

"Well, bring me out a nice plump one. Make sure it's no scrawny bird, understand?"

The young man reappeared shortly with a plump duckling and passed it over to the woman. "This one plump enough for you?"

She pinched its breast, looked under its wings, and stuck her finger up its asshole. "What? This is no Long Island duckling! This is a Massachusetts duckling. Now take it back and get me a Long Island duckling, and no funny business!"

The young man brought her another duckling. "Long Island, guaranteed."

She repeated her examination and stuck her finger up its asshole. "What? Again?! Shame on you trying to fool a nice old lady like me, smart aleck. This is a South Carolina duckling. Now, you got Long Island duckling or not?"

The young man brought her another duckling. She snatched it from his hands, ran her finger up its asshole, and smiled. "Now, *this* is a Long Island duckling. Young man, where you from you should try to fool an old lady like me?"

The young man turned, dropped his pants, mooned the old girl, and said, "I don't know. You tell me!"

Partners

Mort and Sydney had opened their little business five years before and had experienced tremendous success almost instantly. For five years the money came rolling in, and then suddenly the bottom fell out of the hula hoop market. They were flat broke. Poor Mort, always the more volatile, stormed around their office wailing and tearing at his hair, actually pulling out tufts of the greasy stuff and hurling it at the floor like some tribute to his sudden failure. Sydney, on the other hand, paced the floor silently, his hands stuffed deep into his pockets.

"Schmuck! Dodo!" screamed Mort at his partner. "Don't you care? Don't you care about anything? Look at you, calmly strolling around playing with your nuts while I'm going bald here trying not to kill myself!"

"Watch who you're calling a schmuck, Mort," answered Sydney. "I'm tearing my hair out, too, and believe me, it's hurting me a lot worse than it is you!"

Triple-A

A country boy was tootling his rattletrap jalopy along home from town when he came to a lovely young girl sitting by the road in tears, her clothes in tatters. He stopped and asked if he could help her.

"Oh yes, please do," she replied. "Please give me a lift into town. I'm just a mess. This swell fellow brought me out here in a fancy limousine, but when I wouldn't come through, he tried to rape me, then threw me out of the car."

"Oh, my gosh!" said the country boy. "And to a nice little gal like you. Don't that beat all! Come on, hop in."

She jumped in beside him, he turned his jalopy back toward town and started off, bumping and jerking along the rutted country road.

Finally the poor girl couldn't stand the ride a moment longer and said, "Listen, I'm awfully sorry, but you've got to let me out of here."

"But why?" asked the concerned country lad.

"I'd rather be raped in a limo than jerked off in a jalopy!"

San Francisco

"God, what a party," said one of the guys. "I haven't seen so much fucking and sucking since I don't know when."

"Did you see what was going on in the pool house?" asked another. "That Fred must have been on some heavy pharmaceuticals."

"Yeah, yeah, Fred—big deal," said another. "He usually can't even get it up unless there's a camera rolling."

"My dick's so sore it needs a splint," said another.

"What happened?"

"I stepped on it!"

The five of them laughed and lounged back in the redwood hot tub, relaxing in the swirling waters as the sun came up over the bay. Bubbling up from under them, a huge load of milky-white semen broke the surface of the water.

And one of them said, "All right, girls, who farted?!"

Four Nuns in a Jeep

Four nuns driving a combat jeep were killed in a traffic accident with a laser tank on the Santa Monica Freeway. Their senses stunned, they arrived in a bedraggled line before Saint Peter at the Pearly Gates of Heaven.

"Peace, good sisters," said Saint Peter. "If you have any sins, confess them now before you enter through these gates." His voice comforted them, and they were transformed into radiant garments of white, and beatific light shone from around them.

"Good Saint Peter," said Sister Beatrice. "Forgive me, for I have sinned. I have touched a man's penis."

"A small sin for one of such good works," said Saint Peter kindly. "Rinse your hand in that font of holy water and enter into Heaven."

"Ah, good Saint Peter," said Sister Monique. "My sin is far more grievous, for I have held a man's penis in both of my hands."

"Tush, tush," replied Saint Peter. "Dip your hands in that font of holy water and enter the kingdom of Heaven."

Before she could follow Saint Peter's instruction, Sister Angelique ran to the font of holy water, scooped up a handful, and began gargling.

"Sister!" bellowed an outraged Saint Peter. "What in Heaven's name are you doing?"

"Beating Sister Michelle to the holy water before she sits her big ass in it!" she answered.

The First Time

Derek slammed into the house, flushed with excitement, and called, "Mom! Mom, I'm home! Where are you?"

"Here, Derek. What's up?" she asked pleasantly.

"Guess what happened in the gym today. I got laid for the first time!"

Her face tightened into a little ball of outrage. "Not another word, young man! You can discuss this with your father. Now, go to your room and wait. March!"

"Oh, Mom," said a crestfallen Derek.

When his father came home, his mother was waiting like an attack dog. "You'll never believe what your son came home from school with today. I'm just sick. You'd better talk to him. I can't. He's up in his room."

"Gee, son, seems you've got your mother a little bent out of shape. What happened at school today?"

"Aw, Dad," said Derek, close to tears. "I got laid for the first time, that's all."

"You what? You did, really? My son. And only nine years old, too. Listen, Derek, this is pretty serious, but you should keep it just between us men. Don't tell your mother things like this. Okay?"

"You mean, it's all right?" asked Derek, brightening.

"No, I didn't say that. It's not all right. But just don't tell your mother," he said with a wink.

The next day Derek came home from school, marched right past his mother, and went straight to his room. When his father got home, his mother was like a loaded double-barreled shotgun with a hair-fine trigger.

"You go up there and talk to him. He just walked past me like I wasn't there when he came home from school. I just know something is terribly wrong."

"Derek?" said his father, peeking into Derek's room. "Your mother's upset again. Anything happen today? Did you get laid again?"

"Are you crazy?!" answered Derek. "My ass is still sore from yesterday!"

I Had a Dream, Dear

Susan and Bob were all snuggled and comfy in bed for the night, and Bob asked, "What were you so giggly about last night?"

"What do you mean?" asked Susan.

"You were giggling in your sleep. It woke me up."

"Oh, silly, it must have been that weird dream I had. I dreamt I was at a cock auction—isn't that too strange? These great big twelve-inch cocks were ten thousand dollars apiece, and women were snapping them up like crazy. Ten-inch cocks were going for five thousand apiece. Eight-inch cocks were twenty-five hundred. Some women bought two and three. I was hysterical."

"And how much were cocks like mine going for?" asked Bob.

"Oh, ten bucks a gross," answered Susan.

"Gee, that's funny," said Bob. "I had a dream, too, only they were selling cunts. A movie star's cunt went for fifteen thousand, a pin-up girl's for ten thousand."

"What were cunts like mine going for?" asked Susan.

"Are you kidding?" asked Bob. "That's where they held the auction!"

Pass It Along

Lulu had slept with every man on the college football team, singly, in groups, and one particularly pungent night, the whole team at once. The announcement of her upcoming wedding to the college librarian was first met by the team with snickers of disbelief, then hoots of derision, and finally, a vindictive desire to get back at her for cheating on them. They found out the newlywed couple were spending their first night of wedded bliss in a posh hotel in the neighboring town, decided to be a part of it, and sneaked up to their room. Hoisting up the captain of the team so he could spy through the transom, the rest of the team strung out in a line all the way back to the elevator.

"He's kissing her now," reported the captain from his perch atop two sets of shoulders. And the word was whispered back along the line.

"Now he's taking her clothes off," came the report, to be repeated in a whisper, "He's taking her clothes off. . . ." "He's taking her clothes off. . . ." "He's taking her clothes off. . . ."

"He's kissing her titties." And down the corridor this new information flew.

"They've gotten into bed."

"They're in bed" was whispered down the line.

And then the captain of the team heard Lulu say to her new husband, "Oh, lover, you're putting it where no man has ever put it before!"

And the captain reported, "He's fucking her in the ass."

"He's fucking her in the ass. . . ."

"He's fucking her in the ass. . . ."

"He's fucking her in the ass. . . ."

Breakfast Special

Every morning of his life Grandpa Sloane had two eggs over easy with ham, a side of home fries, and four pieces of toast. Since Grandma Sloane passed away several months before, Grandpa Sloane had been eating breakfast out at the Dixie Lee Truck Stop Diner and Billiard Massage Parlor.

Now Dixie Lee was a good old gal, but somehow, hearing old Grandpa Sloane order two eggs over easy with ham, a side of home fries, and four pieces of toast every morning for the past two months had got to her. Just some wild hair up her ass, and when she saw his battered pickup pull in, she scratched his breakfast special from the menu.

When Grandpa Sloane came in and sat at his regular stool at the counter, Dixie Lee sauntered over and said, "I just scratched what you like."

"You did?" said Grandpa Sloane. "Then go wash your hands and get me two eggs over easy with ham, a side of home fries, and four pieces of toast!"

Baby

"I'm pregnant."

His social secretary and companion sat with quiche Lorraine dribbling from his lower lip, hand poised in midreach for the glass of breakfast champagne sparkling in the morning sunshine.

"I know it's hard to believe, but really, George, you're being an absolute gargoyle about it. For God's sake, swallow that quiche or spit it out!"

"But that's impossible," managed George after a mighty swallow.

"Impossible but true. Savoy Tendril, the world's leading gay gossip columnist, pregnant."

"But you're a man!"

"Thank you for noticing. You're sweet. But there's no doubt about it, I'm pregnant."

"Pregnant?"

"Ah, the dawn breaks."

"That's terrible!"

"It's better than a sharp stick in the eye."

"You're sure?"

"Absolutely positively."

"Who's the father?"

"How should I know? Do you think I have eyes in the back of my head?!"

Heavenly Bodies

"Class, which part of the body do you think goes to Heaven first when one dies?"

"The feet, the feet!" yelled little Caryn from the back of the room.

"Caryn, do not shout out like that! Just raise your hand like the other children. Cathy? Which part of the body goes to Heaven first?"

"The brain."

"And why do you think the brain goes first?"

"Because that's where we think all our good thoughts."

"Very good. James? Which part do you think goes to Heaven first?"

"The hands, because we do all our good deeds with our hands."

"It's the feet!" yelled little Caryn.

"Caryn, you simply must raise your hand if you want to be called on."

"It is *too* the feet!" pouted little Caryn.

"All right, Caryn. And why do you think the feet go to Heaven first?"

" 'Cause every time my dad screws my old lady her toes are pointing at the ceiling and she's screaming, 'I'm coming, Lord, I'm coming!' "

The Naked Runner

She heard the key slide into the lock and the lock click. She sat bolt upright in bed, which was a little difficult, considering her afternoon lover was plugging her as hard as he could at the time.

"My God, it's my husband!"

"What?!" said her lover, snapping back to reality.

"My husband, you silly twit! He's home! Quick, the fire escape! You've got to get out of here!"

He leaped the bed in a single bound, sprang through the window, and clambered down the fire escape to the street as fast as he could. Only when he hit the rainy pavement did he realize he was stark naked.

Thinking quickly he fell in step a few paces behind a passing jogger. The jogger acknowledged his presence with a backward glance, did a double take, then said almost casually over his shoulder, "Always jog with your nuts hanging out, do you?"

"Yes, yes," said the naked runner. "Lets the body breathe."

"Always muzzle the hog when you jog?"

"What?"

"The condom you're wearing—always wear a rubber on little Dickie when you jog?"

"No, no," answered the naked runner. "Only when it rains!"

Touchdown!

Having to spend the night at the minister's home wasn't the worst thing that could have happened to the three divinity students. The minister had three dimpled daughters, who had indicated by a well-placed squeeze here, a naughty wink there, and a flash of creamy-white thigh whenever they got the chance that they were available for a little hanky-panky with divinity students not too divine.

"I know, guys," said the hairy little student from Duluth. "As soon as you've scored, call out 'Touchdown!' Not too loud, though. We don't want to wake the reverend and the missus. Now spread out. The last one to score's a Catholic."

They fanned out in the darkened parsonage, creeping from room to room looking for the delights promised by the minister's daughters.

"Touchdown!" broke the stillness of the old parsonage shortly after midnight.

"Touchdown!" again disturbed the silence a little later.

It was well on to one-thirty when the quiet was finally interupted by the third "Touchdown!"

The next morning the third student was asked, "How come it took you so long to score, hotshot?"

"Sorry, fellows," answered the latecomer. "It was a bloody field!"

Contact

"You're never going to believe this, and please don't ask me to explain, but I'm sure I lost one of my contact lenses up my rectum," said Paula.

"How in the world?"

"I asked you not to ask me that. Please, just take

my word for it. It was all quite harmless, I can assure you. And the itching down there is unbearable. I'm sure that's where it got to."

"Drop your pants and lie on the table. On your stomach, please."

The doctor pushed a button and the table folded in the middle, leaving Paula's bottom high in the air. He draped a sheet around her dimpled buttocks so her rosebud anus was the highlight of the show.

"Now you may feel a little discomfort. I'm going to open you up a bit so I can look inside for your lens. Easy now, easy . . . there!"

Paula shrieked.

"I'm sorry, did I hurt you?"

"Oh," giggled Paula, "just a teenie-weenie. Do you see it?"

"No, I don't."

"That's funny, I can see you!"

Christmas Rap

"Okay, Scrooge, what shall we give the mailman, Mr. Ward, for Christmas? Last year we gave him fifteen dollars."

"Give him ten."

"Right. Twenty dollars for Mr. Ward. Last year we gave the babysitter, Becky Sue, ten."

"Give her twenty."

"Right. Ten dollars for Becky Sue. And we gave Mr. Tanaka twenty."

"The gardener?"

"You're right. We'll only give him fifteen. He overfertilized my peace roses. What about Mr.Moses, the milkman?"

"Fuck him."

"Not me, ducks. I fucked him last year!"

Dudley the Dwarf

Dudley wormed his way through the crowded singles'
bar until he was right in front of the six-foot-tall,
statuesque blond beauty.

"Boy, would I love to eat you out," he said in his
insidious, nasty little voice.

She looked around, not believing her ears, but
seeing no one, moved away a few feet and leaned
against a pillar. He elbowed his way after her and
moved in so close his face was almost pressed against
her crotch.

Dudley said, "Come on, baby, I've got a hot tongue
and stamina you wouldn't believe!"

She gave a start, glanced quickly around, shook her
head, then slid around to the other side of the pillar.
Dudley wedged his way through the mob until he was
again in front of her and said, "Don't be shy, baby,
I'm a real eating machine," and put his hand on her
knee.

She gave a yelp, looked down, and saw the dwarf.

"I want to eat you, baby, anytime, anyplace," said
Dudley in his dwarves-have-rights-too voice.

She answered in a tone that would freeze molten
lava, "Well, if you do, and I find out about it . . ."

Sailing, Sailing

The Right Honorable Reverend Raymond didn't
dare tell his wife that the topic of his speech before
the Junior Chamber of Commerce that Thursday was
to be sex. She'd never come to grips with the subject
and it apparently left her cold. Any mention of sex
met with her instant disapproval, so he told her the

speech was about sailing, to which she responded, "That's nice, dear."

Mrs. Raymond happened to be downtown shopping that Thursday and ran into one of the Jaycees, who had just come from the luncheon.

"Afternoon, Mrs. Raymond," he said, tipping his hat.

"Why, Harry Crotch! What a pleasant surprise. And how did my husband's speech go today?"

"Quite interesting, Mrs. Raymond, a real roof raiser. I'd never have guessed he was such an expert in the field. What a man! He certainly knew the ins and outs of his subject matter, if you know what I mean. And what a lucky woman you are to have a husband with such insight and vigor," he said, winking lasciviously.

"Insight and vigor? What on earth are you talking about? He only did it twice! The first time made him sick, and the second time blew his hat off!"

Elizabetta and Rastaman

"Elizabetta, how you be likin' that little yellow bird I done give to you?"

"Oh, Rastaman, I likes him so fine. He be singin' so sweet."

"And how you be likin' them shiny drop earrings I done give to you?"

"Oh, Rastaman, I likes them so fine. They shine so gold, just like that little yellow bird's song."

"And how you be likin' them brand-new panty hose I done give to you?"

"Oh, Rastaman, I likes them so fine. Only every time I farts I blows my shoes off!"

Man's Best Friend?

It wasn't so bad when Tom got washed up on a desert island with nothing but a nanny goat and a dog. Fresh fruit and fish were plentiful. And he had the nanny goat for fresh milk and the dog for companionship. After several months Tom was rested, tanned, in great physical shape, and horny as a four-dicked donkey in July.

One day as he milked the nanny goat, who he had affectionately named Diane, his mind wandered as he firmly pulled her warm teats. Before he realized what he was doing, he grabbed her by the haunches and stuck her for all he was worth. Poor Diane's frightened bleating roused the dog, and before Tom could complete his dire act of abandon, the dog nipped him by the seat and pulled him off.

"Thanks, dog," said Tom dejectedly, and he walked off down the lonely beach. But the next time Tom tried to rape poor Diane it was premeditated and desperate. Again his faithful dog pulled him away from the dastardly deed. Tom began to hate the dog. Any attempt to sate his dark lust with the nanny goat was stopped by the dog, who appeared mysteriously and instantly to protect her.

One day, a pale, beautiful woman was washed up on the beach, more dead than alive. Tom nursed her back to health and vitality, tending to her every need gently and with kindness.

Out of gratitude for Tom's bringing her back to life, the now-golden, beautiful woman said, "Tom, if it weren't for you I'd be dead now. You're a kind, tender, and very attractive man. Is there any way I can repay your kindness and express my gratitude?"

"There sure is," answered Tom. "Hold that damned dog!"

Toilet Trained

"Irving!" Sadie screamed from the bathroom. "Irving, wake up, you miserable rat! Irving! Get in here!" And she screamed and screamed.

"What is it?" said Irving, bleary-eyed from sleep. "My God! Sadie! What are you doing in the toilet?"

"I'm sticking in the toilet, that's what I'm doing, you *meshuggeneh gonif!* I told you not to leave the seat up in the middle of the night. Get me out of here!"

But try as he might, tugging on her hands, grabbing her around the waist, yanking and hoisting, he couldn't get her unstuck.

"Oh, Sadie," said poor Irving, wringing his hands. "What am I going to do? I can't get you out!"

"If you ever do, I'm going to kill you! I promise you that, Irving!"

"Rodriguez! I'll get the super to help me!"

And then she really screamed. "Rodriguez?! I'm naked. He can't see me naked!"

Poor Irving was so rattled he tossed her his yarmulke. "Here, cover yourself with this!" And he was off to get Rodriguez.

When they returned, Sadie was still firmly wedged in the bowl with her arms concealing her breasts and the yarmulke tucked between her legs.

"Well, what do you think, Rodriguez? Can you get her out?" asked Irving.

"Yeah, yeah, I can get her out," replied Rodriguez. "But the rabbi's a goner for sure!"

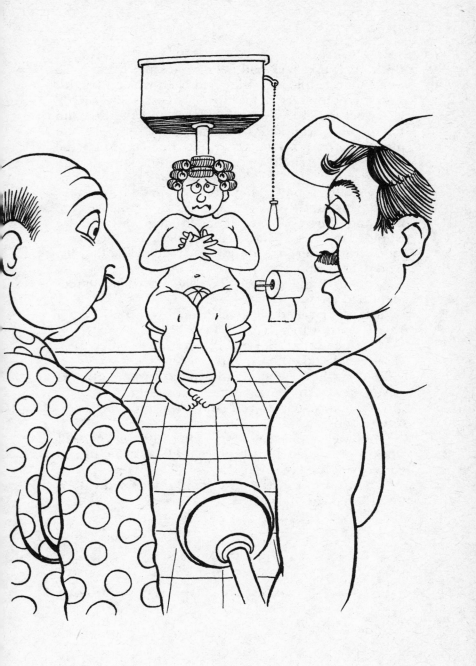

Layoff

Both Mary and Jack had been loyal employees. Even more than employees, they had been trusted friends since Arnold started his tiny business some fifteen years before. But times were hard and the demand for elk-horn wine flasks had fallen off. One of them had to be let go. Jack was the craftsman, Mary the bookkeeper. Arnold could cover either job. How to decide which to let go? Flip a coin? Ask them?

The water cooler. They both stopped at the water cooler during the day. Arnold decided to leave it to fate and thirst. The first one to the water cooler would have to go. He sat at his desk waiting like a mournful spider, dreading the arrival of the first fly. And in came Mary.

Arnold struggled to his feet, shocked that the moment had arrived.

"Mary," he called. Then clearing his throat, "May I have a word with you?"

Mary peered at him myopically through her thick glasses and said, "You sign the checks."

"Yes, yes I do. That's kind of what I wanted to talk to you about. How many years has it been?"

"Too many," answered Mary through her cold-clogged nose.

"Yes, well, you see, Mary, after fifteen years of working so closely together, well, I'll be straight with you. I've got to lay you or Jack off."

"Then go jack off! I just came in for a drink of water!" replied Mary.

Tit for Tat

The voluptuous redhead perched on her bar stool like a lonely lady looking to take a fall for the right guy with the right come-on. Marvin wrote, "May I buy you a drink?" on a scrap of paper, made a little airplane out of the paper, and landed it right in front of her. She smiled at him, read the note, and shouted loud enough for everyone in the bar to hear, "You want me to come to your hotel room?!"

Marvin was mortified and, trying to become invisible, sank his head down between his shoulders. After his total despair abated he ventured a look at the redhead, and she tossed him a dazzling smile. This puzzled Marvin, and he thought perhaps she realized from his abject embarrassment that he meant no harm, so he asked the bartender to serve her another martini, on him.

When the redhead realized who the martini was from, she again shouted loud enough to rouse the dead, "You want to undress me?!"

Marvin turned to jelly, sank six inches lower on his stool, and audibly whimpered with public shame. He was wondering how long a bottle of aspirin would take to kill him when the bartender put a note in front of him and said, "It's from the redhead broad."

Marvin read the note: "Just testing you. Sorry." He turned to the redhead, who flashed him another heart-melting smile, and shouted as loud as he could, "You want fifty dollars?!"

The Ant and the Elephant

Leila the elephant was walking down the jungle path, and she got a thorn in her foot. Ouch! Oh my, how it hurt. She tried to remove it with her trunk, but her trunk was just too big to grasp the small thorn. Each step she took brought fresh elephant tears to her eyes.

"Oh, Mr. Ant!" she called, espying an ant on the path. "I've got this teeny-tiny thorn in my foot, and I can't get it out. Please, please, I'd do anything if you could remove it for me."

"Anything?" asked Mr. Ant.

"Yes, anything. It's so painful I think I shall go mad. And you know how bad a mad elephant can be!"

She lifted her foot, and Mr. Ant jumped and clung to the thorn, yanking and heaving, until finally it slid free of Leila the elephant's foot.

"Ohhhhhh," what a sigh of relief Leila sighed. "Mr. Ant, thank you, thank you, thank you. Now what can I do for you?"

"Well," replied Mr. Ant, "there's a terrible number of anteaters around, and, well, frankly, there aren't that many Miss Ants, if you know what I mean. Could I rip off a little piece?"

Leila blushed as deeply as a lady elephant can blush and said coyly, "Well, yes, I suppose so."

Mr. Ant made the long trip up one of her back legs and stood before her gaping sex. With a look of total bliss on his little ant face he leaped in and took her where she stood.

Titwoe the monkey watched all of this from his perch high in a coconut tree and became hysterical with laughter watching the ant and the elephant below, so hysterical in fact, that he knocked a coconut out of the tree, and it landed smack on Leila the elephant's head.

"Ouch!" she cried.

"That's right, bitch, take it all!" cried Mr. Ant.

Coming of Age

For his Confirmation, Salvatore's father gave him a shiny silver pistol. For his Bar Mitzvah, Benjamin's father gave him a gold watch.

Salvatore and Benjamin were best friends and each admired the other's "growing-up" gift. In fact, each admired the other's gift so much they decided to trade.

Later that week at the dinner table, Salvatore's father noticed the gold watch and said, "Salvatore, that's a handsome watch."

"Thank you, Papa," said Salvatore.

"How'd you come by that fine watch, Salvatore?" asked his father.

"Uh-oh," said Salvatore.

" 'Uh-oh?' What do you mean, 'uh-oh'? You didn't steal it, did you? *Mama mia,* you stole the watch!" said Salvatore's father, snatching at him across the table to wring his neck.

"No, no! I didn't steal it! I traded Benjamin for it. Honest!"

"Then Benjamin's a fool!" answered his father. "What'd you give him for such a watch?"

"I traded my silver pistol."

"Your silver pistol?! Oh, fine, just fine!"

"I have no use for the silver pistol, Papa. But the gold watch tells me the time!" explained Salvatore.

"Oh, sure, sure!" raged his father. "What will you do when you're married and you come home and find your wife in bed with another man? Push back your sleeve, tap your watch, and say, 'Ah, ah, ah! Time's up?!' "

The Physical

Big Lenny Aitch was standing in line in his under-wear with a thousand other guys having his induction physical for the army. He'd been measured, weighed, his eyes tested, he'd peed in a bottle, had blood taken, bent over and spread his cheeks, coughed, and now the army doctor was examining his penis for venereal disease.

The doctor held Big Lenny's heavy hose in one hand and slid the foreskin back with the other. He'd had a long day of penis after penis and lost track of where he was and repeated the motion again and again.

Big Lenny tapped him on the head and said, "Hey, Doc, if you're doing that for the army, go right ahead. But if you're doing it for me, could you move a little faster, please?"

Stars and Stripes Forever

He married the ugly troll for her money. What a shock when her father insisted he sign an agreement stipulating he get her pregnant within the first year or the marriage would be annulled. Ugh, he thought, how am I ever going to make love to her?

"Son," said her father, "I know her face is a mess, but the body's not too bad. Cover her face with the flag if you want to stuff the tuna, and fuck for Old Glory. I want a grandson. Make a game of it. She's dim-witted enough to think it's fun."

And it worked. With her face covered with the flag, he could pretend she was anyone he liked, and she seemed to think the game cute, patriotic, or whatever.

Shortly after the honeymoon, he was hanging a picture in the den with his monosyllabic, grossly plain wife helping. Perched atop the ladder, he asked her for a nail.

"Da . . . da . . . da . . . nail!" She reasoned out his request and got him a nail.

Then he asked for a hammer.

"Da . . . da . . . da . . . hammer!" And she got him the hammer.

As he was driving the nail, he smashed his thumb and screamed in painful rage, "FUCK!"

"Da . . . da . . . da . . . FLAG!" And she rushed off to get him the flag.

Monkey Glands

Poor Milty had his testicles crushed when his trailer truck jackknifed on the George Washington Bridge. Fortunately he was rushed to Mount Cyanide Hospital where the most advanced experiments in testicle transplants were being done. When he awoke that evening in the recovery room after hours of surgery, all he was told was that he was fine, just fine. The next day his doctor told him he had the first testicle transplant in history and had every chance of recovery. He wasn't told the testicles he had received were from a chimpanzee donor.

A year later his wife was giving birth to their first child. Milty paced impatiently back and forth in the maternity waiting room chain-smoking and searching for body lice in his chest hair. Finally, the doctor poked his head in and beckoned to Milty. Milty rushed over and said, "Well, Doc?"

"Congratulations, Mr. Jones, you have a healthy, energetic baby!"

"But what is it, a boy or a girl?" asked Milty eagerly.

"Not so fast, Mr. Jones, we'll know that just as soon as we can get the little monkey down from the chandelier!"

A Bird in the Bush

Hank really had Sonya going now. First they just strolled along the lakeshore enjoying the beautiful afternoon. Then they sat in a shaded spot watching the ducks swimming and feeding, bobbing their little heads under the water and popping their feathery little behinds up in the air. When Hank pointed out how much their feathery little behinds reminded him of Sonya's downy little cranny, the symbology got to both of them, and soon they were necking up a storm, feeling, petting, squeezing, and unzipping. Realizing he'd better relieve his bladder before things got out of hand and into Sonya, as it were, Hank excused himself and hurried into the bushes to take a mighty leak.

"Jesus Fucking Christ!" roared an irate voice from the bushes. "Who the hell you think you're pissing on?!"

"Come on, man, watch your language!" said Hank. "There's a lady present."

"Oh, really!" answered the voice. "Who you think I'm fucking in here, King Kong?!"

Judgment

On the final judgment day all the souls of Heaven and earth were in a line stretching into infinity before the Almighty. Many were paired as they had been in their lives, and the Almighty asked one man, "Was this woman your only mate, faithful and true, throughout your lifetime?"

"Yes, Lord," answered the man.

"And what was her name?"

"Candy, Lord."

"You both shall be cast into the void and not know the eternal sweetness of Heaven, as you are a creature of gluttony. Even your wife's name shows this."

When the Almighty heard the next man's wife was named Penny, the Almighty said, "You both shall be cast into the eternal void, as you are a creature of avarice and greed. Even your wife's name shows this."

Further down the line, Melvin whispered to his wife, "Let's get out of here, Fanny. We haven't got a prayer!"

D.W.I.

"All right, lady, pull it over," said the motorcycle cop to Harriet.

When she'd brought her car to a stop and he'd parked his cycle, he strolled to her window and said, "Driver's license and registration, please. Take them out of your wallet."

"Officer," Harriet tried to explain, "I don't understand. This is the second time I've been stopped today, and I'm an excellent driver."

"Looks like a clear case of D.W.I. to me," replied the officer.

"That's what the other officer said, but I don't drink, so I certainly can't be driving while intoxicated. Fiddle-dee-dee! He made me take your silly breathalizer test anyway. I passed, so he let me go with a warning."

At that moment the officer realized his fly was open and reached to zip up.

And Harriet said, "Oh, come on now, not another breathalizer test!"

Winston Farthington Gales

Winston Farthington Gales was lying on his deathbed with his adoring wife, Muffy, at his side.

"Muffy? Still here?"

"Yes, Binky dearest, still here."

"How long has it been?"

"Forty-two years, Binkums."

"Forty-two years. That long. Back at Harvard you cheered me on when I captained the debate team and consoled me when we lost to Yale."

"Yes, Binky love."

"And when we represented America in the Yacht Cup Race, I capsized the boat and we almost drowned."

"Yes, Binkums."

"And when I was having that affair with the Spanish dancer, you stuck by me when she got pregnant and wouldn't settle out of court."

"Yes, dearest."

"And when I made those lousy investments and wiped out your inheritance, you stuck with me all the way."

"But of course, love."

"And when Biff, our son, my only son, came back from Casablanca with a sex change and I wanted to kill myself, you knocked the pistol from my hand."

"Oh, Binky, Binkums."

"And now I'm lying here, still a young man, dying of cancer, and you're still by my side."

"Oh, Binky, Binkums, love."

"You know what, Muffy?"

"What?"

"Lean closer."

"Yes, Binkums."

"Muffy, you're a fucking jinx!"

Movement

"I think I'm running a slight fever, Doctor, but perhaps not. I don't know, I'm just not feeling myself. Do you think I'm coming down with something?"

The doctor checked her pulse, blood pressure, and temperature, weighed her, and measured her height. While studying her chart meticulously, he was mentally flipping a coin between two aspirins and rest, a shot of vitamin B_{12}, or a hundred thousand units of penicillin.

Then he asked, "How are your bowel movements?"

"I beg your pardon!"

"I mean, are you regular and what's the consistency of your stool?"

"Regular and firm. In fact, I'm so regular you could set your watch by my morning 7:45. Seven forty-five sharp! Each and every morning."

"Well, pooh, pooh, pooh. Looks like a big dose of penicillin for you."

"Very funny. Ha, ha, ha!"

He actually relished pumping the hundred thousand units of penicillin into her flaccid backside. He especially loved the way she bit her lip to keep from flinching.

As the penicillin began to work its way through her system, two germs became alarmed.

Jerry Germ cried, "Oh no, it's penicillin! What'll we do?"

Joey Germ answered, "I don't know about you, kiddo, but I'm catching the morning 7:45 out of here!"

The $50.00 Frog

Jeanne glanced at all the irresistible little creatures in the pet-shop window she passed on her way to work. But when she got to the office, what stuck in her mind was the average-looking frog with the fifty-dollar price tag on its cage. Fifty dollars for a frog? Someone had to be kidding.

That evening on her way home, she dropped into the pet shop and asked the owner, "What's the come-on with the fifty-dollar frog in the window?"

"It's no come-on. That frog's worth well over fifty dollars. I can see you're intelligent, so I'll tell you that frog can please any woman better than any man ever could. There it's out. Yell at me. Call me a shit, but that frog could make Elizabeth Taylor forget about men."

"You're a shit. I'll take the frog."

That evening after bathing, scenting her body, and donning her most alluring negligee, Jeanne lounged back on her bed and opened the frog's cage. Half an hour later she drifted off to sleep, but the frog hadn't moved.

Figuring the frog just needed to get used to his new surroundings, Jeanne repeated her ritual the next evening. The frog croaked, but never moved.

"You shit!" she screamed into the phone at the pet-shop owner. "The fucking frog isn't!"

"Don't move. Stay just as you are. I'll be right over," he answered.

"Where's the frog?" he asked when Jeanne let him into the apartment.

"Follow me," said Jeanne, leading him off to the bedroom. When she turned around the pet-shop owner was completely naked and sporting a quality erection. "What on earth?!"

And the pet-shop owner said, "Now, watch real close, frog! This is the last time I'm going to show you this!"

The War Years

"The war years were very brutal for our small convent. The sisters suffered severe tribulation during those dark days when the Germans swept through our small community and raped every single one of us, except for Sister Anne.

"And then the barbaric Russians drove the Germans back and raped every single one of us, except for Sister Anne.

"And then the Americans came with their smiles and chocolate bars and savage weapons and raped every single one of us, except for Sister Anne."

"Why wasn't Sister Anne ever raped?"

"She didn't want to."

The Showstopper

"Hey! Kenny! Right? Okay? You know? Lighten up. Okay? I mean, I don't understand how you always get the beautiful women! Hey! Sorry, I must be stupid or something. How do you do it? Explain it to me. Hey, now don't get me wrong. I think you're a great guy and all that.

"I mean, you're not that good-looking. Hey, sorry, no offense meant. But let's face it, there's good-looking and then there's good-looking. Know what I mean? You dress real nice. I mean, you know, you're not setting any trends. But that's what I like about you. You're quiet. You know? So how do you do it? How do you always get the beautiful women? I'm dyin' here, you know?"

"I find a quiet bar."
"Yeah?"
"I get a table in the corner."
"Yeah?"
"I order a bottle of wine.
"Yeah?"
"The rest is a piece of cake."
"Piece of cake? What cake? What? What?"
"I lick my eyebrows."

Suicide

Old Mama Leoni was depressed. She was more depressed than depressed. She was really depressed. She knew it was a mortal sin to kill herself, but she was determined to do it, and to do it right the first time. It would be too depressing to botch the job, so she went to her doctor.

"Doctor, I'm going to kill myself, and I want to be sure exactly where my heart is."

Her doctor scolded her for thinking such bad thoughts, gave her a prescription for a tranquilizer, and tried to send her home.

"I don't want to hear any more of this suicide nonsense. You're a fine woman with a fine family and everything to live for. Now, enjoy life. And take one of the pills I prescribed for you if you're feeling bad about things."

"Doctor, where's my heart?"

"Directly beneath your left breast."

And true to her word, Mama Leoni went home and blew off her left kneecap!

The Casting Couch

Two young Hollywood hopefuls were having lunch in the studio commissary.

"This extra work sucks the big wazoo," said Linda, "but it does pay the rent."

"I've been third bimbo to the left in so many B movies I could puke," agreed Fran.

"How'd you make out with that director last night?" asked Linda.

"I gave him everything I've got," replied Fran. "Wish I'd had the clap—I'd have given him that, too. The prick wasn't even good for dinner. Directors!" said Fran in disgust. "Give a girl a drink, and they want to fuck you till Tuesday!"

"Listen, Fran, I think I've got crab lice," said Linda. "How can I get rid of them?"

"That's no problem. Just smear some Paris green in your bush."

Several days later they met on the saloon set for a Western, and Fran asked, "Hey, Linda, did the Paris green kill your crabs?"

"Sure did," answered Linda, "and a couple of directors, too!"

The Rick-and-Rose Show

"Rick, darling, is there anything special I can do for you? After twenty-five years of happy marriage, I just don't know what else to do for you."

"Well, all the times I've made love to you, I've never felt I was good enough to make you moan."

"Moan? What moan?"

"You know—moan. Like my lovemaking's touched you to the very depths of your being."

"Moan? What are you talking about, moan? I should have to moan?"

"Never mind."

"No, no! You want I should moan, I'll moan. Just tell me when."

"How can I do that?"

"Just say, 'Rose, moan,' so I should know it's time. I'll moan."

That night after the anniversary celebration, they were both a little tipsy, very happy, and feeling romantic. Rick embraced Rose, nibbled her ear, and licked her neck.

"Now?" asked Rose.

"No, not now," he answered. He lay her back on the bed and slipped her negligee off her shoulders and kissed her neck and moved down to her familiar breasts with his lips parted and his tongue kissing little butterfly kisses.

"Now?" asked Rose.

"No, not now," he answered. He pushed her negligee aside, kissed, nibbled, and licked his way down to the fuzzy thicket that covered the love canal he had traveled so many times before. He nuzzled his face into her bush until his tongue could enter her. As he tenderly pulled her lush lips apart, he said, "Now, Rose, now."

"Ohhhhh," moaned Rose, "such a line at the supermarket today, you wouldn't believe. Never mind the checkout girl wasn't even wearing a bra. And the traffic . . ."

Soup du Jour

When Alan's soup was served, he noticed the waiter's thumb was in the bowl.

"I'm sorry, waiter, I've changed my mind," said Alan. "I prefer the New England clam chowder, not the Manhattan clam chowder."

"Okeydokey," said the waiter amiably. When he returned with the New England clam chowder, Alan saw the waiter's thumb was again firmly planted in the soup.

"Waiter," said Alan, "perhaps I should go with the consommé. Fewer calories."

"Anything you say," replied the waiter, and he trotted back to the kitchen. But when he returned with the consommé, again his thumb was in the soup.

"Forget the soup, waiter, and please send the manager over."

"Yes, sir," said the waiter, smartly turning on his heel.

When the manager came to the table, Alan said, "What the devil is going on here? I've ordered three different soups, and each time the waiter serves it with his thumb in the bowl!"

"I'm terribly sorry, sir. You see, he has an arthritic thumb, and he keeps it in the soup for the warmth."

"Well, tell him to stick it up his ass!"

"Yes, sir, that's where he keeps it when it's not in the soup!"

Wayward Nurse

Dr. Thumbs was making his rounds of B ward when a middle-aged, hospital-gowned patient dashed past, his gown flapping open in the back like an aging pederast's siren song. Then Nurse Wayward dashed past Dr. Thumbs, carrying a pot of boiling water, in hot pursuit of the fleeing male patient.

"Nurse!" shouted Dr. Thumbs after the double apparition of disaster.

"Not now, Doctor, just following orders!" called back Nurse Wayward as she rounded the corridor corner with her pot of boiling water.

My God, thought Dr. Thumbs, must she get everything ass backwards?

"Nurse!" shouted Dr. Thumbs, chasing down the corridor after her. As he rounded the corner, he saw the hunter and the hunted in the distance.

"Nurse! Stop! I told you to prick his boil!"

The Family Name

"Look, Pop, I'm sorry to call you at such a late hour, but I'm in big trouble. You see I got this girl pregnant, and I need ten thousand dollars to keep her quiet."

"What? You idiot! Ten thousand dollars! What do you think I am, made of money?"

"Pop, listen, I'm sorry, but if I don't pay her the money, she's going to spread the family name all over the papers. It'll be a terrific scandal, and Mom could never stand that."

"All right, all right, I'll send the money. But make her sign a paper! You hear me? Make her sign a paper!"

A month or so later, his other son came home from school on vacation and said, "You have to help me, Pop."

"Help? No help. I'm ruined already."

"But, Pop, it's this girl. She claims it's my baby. I've got to pay her ten thousand dollars or she's going to file a paternity suit."

"Idiot, what've you been doing, taking stupid lessons from your brother?"

"But, Pop, the family name! Think of the scandal!"

Totally cowed, the father paid. No sooner had his young son left when his sixteen-year-old daughter came to him.

"Daddy . . ." said the apple of his eye.

"Yes, Princess?"

"I'm pregnant!" And she began weeping pitifully.

"Hurrah!" cheered the overjoyed father. "Business is picking up at last!"

Sea Horse

"He's a fine animal," said Mr. Dicknose. "How much do you want for him?"

"Twenty dollars."

"Twenty dollars? It's a deal." Mr. Dicknose knew a bargain when he saw one and had no sympathy for any rube who didn't know the value of horse flesh. When he got the beautiful, molasses-colored stallion home, he saddled him and took him out for a ride. The stallion handled beautifully, his taut muscles rippling under his sleek coat. Mr. Dicknose was well pleased with his purchase. But when they reached the old wooden bridge over the small river that wound through his property, the horse bolted, leaped the rail, unseating Mr. Dicknose, and plunged into the river. Mr. Dicknose swam to the bank and watched as his beautiful stallion thrashed about wildly in the water, lunging this way and that until he was exhausted and dragged himself out of the river.

Mr. Dicknose led the stallion the three miles back to the barn. When they came to the large fish pond near the barn, the horse wrenched free from Mr. Dicknose and threw himself into the pond and writhed about in the water. Mr. Dicknose walked on to the barn, sent one of his hands back for the horse, and made a phone call.

"What's the story with this crazy stallion you sold me? No wonder you only wanted twenty dollars for him. He goes completely bonkers whenever he's around water."

"Yeah, I know," was the reply. "He only fucks fish!"

Bad Dog

Shelley was seated on the couch with her good dog Deenie lying on the floor beside her when Terry took her hand in his and popped the all-important question. She accepted his proposal of marriage, and in ecstasy he moved to embrace her in his arms and ripped off a real cheese-cutter.

"Deenie!" shouted Shelley at the poor innocent dog. "Now get out of here!"

Deenie looked up, abashed at her mistress's tone, while Terry thought, Geez, how embarrassing! Luckily the dog was taking the rap for that spicy Mexican dinner he'd eaten, and all's fair in love and war. But as he again moved to smother Shelley with his ardor, he again cut the cheese, this round much riper than the previous.

"Deenie! Yuck! Go on, get!" cried Shelley.

Deenie lifted her head and looked at her mistress with those big, brown, I-didn't-do-anything eyes.

"Aw, she can't help it," said Terry kindly as he again made his big move to seal their engagement with a kiss.

"Oh cripes, Deenie!" admonished Terry when he again polluted the atmosphere with a bang. "Really!"

"Yeah, Deenie, really," said Shelley. "You better get out of here before he shits all over you!"

Fantasy

Laurie Naked was having lunch with Tara O'Hara, and oddly enough, they were discussing their sexual fantasies. Tara O'Hara was definitely into gang rapes, particularly if the gang was sailors, but it wasn't really much good unless they left their little white caps on. Laurie Naked wasn't interested in group sex, but she did have a fancy for cowboy boots and spurs and liked to yell, "Ride 'em, cowboy!" at the right moment.

"Do you ever fantasize about black men?" asked Tara O'Hara.

"No, never," answered Laurie Naked. "But I did dream about Patrick the other night."

"Patrick!" said Tara O'Hara, her eyes growing wide and turning dark. "Patrick at work? Oh, Laurie, he's gorgeous! What happened?"

"I dreamed I was lying in bed asleep and a sound at the window woke me. But I kept still and opened my eyes just a little bit so I could peek through my lashes. The window opened, and Patrick climbed in."

"Oh my gosh!" said Tara O'Hara. "Was he naked?"

"No, not then. But he was hot and sweaty and looked mad. Then he saw me and took off all his clothes."

"Did he have a big one?" asked Tara O'Hara.

"Jesus tits, Tara! Would you let me tell it?"

"Well, what's the point of fantasizing if he didn't have a big one?"

"I wasn't fantasizing! I was dreaming. And yes, he had a big one. It was as big as a man's forearm with the fist balled up."

"That's the way I like it, uh-huh."

"Well, I was really scared, so I sat up in bed and said, 'What are you going to do with that big thing?' "

"What'd he say?"

"He looked kind of surprised and said, 'Don't ask me, lady. It's your dream!' "

Toot! Toot!

"But, conductor, you don't understand! We're on our honeymoon. We just got married today!"

"What's the matter, Bobbyboy?"

"Sugar lamb, baby love, we've got separate berths on opposite sides of the aisle. Things are all screwed up. Conductor, can't you put us together?"

"Sorry, sir, the sleeping berths are all full."

"Oh no, Bobbyboy!" wailed sugar lamb baby love. "Not on our honeymoon!"

"Hush now, angel pie, don't you fret," he said intimately. "I've got something long enough and hard enough so you can crawl over to my berth."

And some smart aleck behind them said, "Yeah, but how's she gonna get back?!"

Mirror, Mirror

Lady M. stood back admiring the antique rococo mirror the workmen had just finished hanging in her boudoir, looked her reflection up and down, and said, "Boy, would I like a pair of forty-four D bazooms."

The flash of lightning and clap of thunder startled her half out of her wits, but when she regained her composure, she was startled even more by what she saw in the mirror. Threatening to burst the seams of her silk blouse were the biggest pair of breasts she'd ever seen. First she was aghast at the change, but a giggle began to ricochet in her head until she was dancing around the room singing, "Hey, look me over, tell me what you see. Ain't these the prettiest balloons that you did ever see?"

Lord M. had hardly the time to hear her story about the stupid mirror and barely noticed or cared about her expanded chest. But late that night as Lady M. lay snoring in her canopied bed, Lord M. tiptoed into her boudoir and stood naked before the mirror. Thinking about the luscious new girl in the steno pool, he whispered, "Mirror, mirror, make my penis touch the floor."

A flash of lightning, a clap of thunder, and his legs shrank three feet!

Keeping Cool

Hubert came home unexpectedly one afternoon and found his wife naked in a rumpled bed with a cigar burning in the ash tray beside her and the bedroom window open with the curtains flapping. He looked out the window, then ran to the kitchen and looked out the back window. He saw a man in the alley cinching his belt, and in a brute rage Hubert picked up the refrigerator and tossed it out the window, hitting the man and killing him instantly. When he realized what he had done, he pulled out his revolver and shot himself dead. Hubert was a policeman.

At the Pearly Gates Hubert told his story to Saint Peter, who was sympathetic, but sent him to Hell anyway.

The next man before Saint Peter explained, "I really don't know why I'm here. I'd just finished repairing a telephone line and was walking down the alley tightening my belt 'cause I've lost so much weight on my wife's new diet. I looked up just as this refrigerator came hurtling down at me. It must have hit me, 'cause here I am."

Saint Peter was very sympathetic, but sent the telephone repairman to purgatory to contemplate how not to be in the right place at the wrong time.

The next man in line said, "You're never going to believe this, but all I was doing was cooling off in a refrigerator!"

Marvelous Mavis

"Hey, baby, slip into this genuine leather upholstery. Oooh, you look good tonight. I like a lady to look fine when she goes out with Marvelous Mavis. I bet you never been in a boss car like this before, have you? Check out that genuine teak inlay dash. Now I'm telling you, this car is something else!"

Marvelous pulled away from the curb at eighty miles an hour.

"I like my women full-figured, so pick out anything your little heart desires. Don't worry about how much it costs—this restaurant's so expensive they don't even put prices on the menu. You never have been in a place as fancy as this, have you?"

After dinner, Marvelous couldn't find the keys to his car, so they took a cab to his apartment.

"Just get comfortable. Marvelous Mavis *does* have the greatest pad on the West Coast. Check out that view. Look at those stars, make a wish, and I bet it's me. Hey, baby, relax. Don't be all tense just because you never saw a place as grand as this before."

Marvelous took off all his clothes.

"I don't want to scare you, baby, but this is me, all natural, the real Marvelous Mavis. Did you ever see this much beautiful skin on one man? Now you do have to admit I have a handcarved body. And did you ever see anything like this?"

"Yes," she answered. "A couple of times. It looks just like a cock, only it's a whole lot smaller!"

Samurai

"I don't mean to insult your greatness, Samurai-san, but would you give me an example of your skill?"

The samurai said, "Do you see that fly circling overhead?" And in a flash he drew his sword and bisected the fly, the two pieces dropping at the feet of the American journalist. "But if you want to interview the greatest living samurai in Japan, you should not waste your time with me. My father is far greater samurai than I."

The American journalist got the directions to the father's house, which turned out to be a small castle in the foothills.

"Samurai-san, your son has said you are the greatest living samurai and sent me to speak to you. Would you please give me an example of your greatness?"

The father samurai said, "Do you see that fly circling overhead?" And in an instant he drew his sword and quartered the fly, the four pieces dropping at the feet of the American journalist. "But if you want to interview the greatest samurai in the twentieth century, you should speak to my father, not I. My father is truly the greatest living samurai."

When the American journalist arrived at the grandfather samurai's house, he was impressed with the remoteness and grandness of the mountaintop castle.

"Surely you must be the greatest living samurai, as your son and grandson have said. Great Samurai-san, please show me your skill."

The ancient, wizened samurai said in a cracking voice, "Do you see that fly circling overhead?" And faster than the eye could see he drew his sword, slashed the air, and sheathed his sword.

"But great Samurai-san, the fly has flown away."

"Ah, yes," said the ancient samurai. "The fly has flown away. But he'll never fuck again!"

Import/Export

"Daddy, what do they do with all the little foreskins from the baby boys when they're circumcised?" asked his preteen daughter.

A bit taken aback, her father asked, "Where did you hear about circumcision?"

"Mrs. O'Tooley told us in hygiene class at school," she answered.

"Oh, she did, did she? Well, you see, prettypot, all the little foreskins are packed up in a big crate and shipped to Ireland."

"Why do they send them there?"

"So they can plant them in the ground and water and care for them, and they grow up to be big Irish pricks."

"Why do they do that?"

"So they can ship them back to us and make New York City cops out of them!"

Four-Alarm Fire

"And how old was your husband, Mrs. Twiddleclit?" asked the constable.

"Eighty-two and a fortnight," replied the teenage widow.

"Begging your pardon, ma'am, but did anything

unusual happen to bring about the fatal attack?"

"Well, yes and no. We were making love when it happened."

"Hrmmph!" said the constable clearing his throat. "It's a pity these older blokes, well, meaning no disrespect, ma'am, but your husband, God rest his soul, probably shouldn't have been taking on such a young wife as yourself, if you get my meaning."

"Constable, my husband was as much of a johnny-root as a man half his age—no, a quarter his age. Why, we made love regular-like, to the pealing of the church-tower bells. He liked to make love to the pealing of the bells. Ring in, ring out, ring in, ring out."

Blushing scarlet, the constable said, "Yes, well, of course."

" 'Ring in, ring out, ring in, ring out, oh, ye bells of heaven.' That was his favorite song."

"Hmmm. You said something unusual happened?"

"Well, yes and no. We were making love as usual to the ringing of the bells—ring in, ring out—"

"I get the picture, Mrs. Twiddleclit. Can we get on with it?"

"Yes, of course, Constable. We was making love, keeping time with the bells, like I said, when that four-alarmer broke out down the street."

"Yes?"

"Well, don't you see? It must of been that clanging fire truck what done him in!"

Eau de Parfum

"My dear, excuse me," inquired the exquisitely dressed woman in the elevator of the exquisitely dressed woman standing beside her, "what is that heavenly scent you're wearing?"

"Oh, why thank you. It's 'Aphrobrosia' by Prince Poncielli, two hundred dollars a gram," answered the elegant mannequin. "And I notice you're wearing something enchantingly sweet. What might it be?"

"Ah, it's Cerubini's 'Je suis Titania,' two hundred and twenty dollars a gram."

At that moment a squeaky bang was heard, and a pervasively sick odor filled the elevator.

"Good God in Heaven," said one of the haute-couture females to the other, "what was that?"

And a voice from the rear of the elevator answered, "It's a broccoli, seventy-nine cents a pound!"

Golf Pro

"Oh, honey, I'm so happy we're married at last. I'm going to be good for you. I really am."

"I know, Betty darling, and I'm going to be good for you, too."

"I'm not a virgin. You're not angry are you? I should have told you before, but I was afraid."

"Hey, we're both of age. You didn't think I was a virgin, did you?"

"But you're a man—that's different. I want to tell you everything. I really do, make a fresh start. His name was Roscoe Simms."

"Not *the* Roscoe Simms, the golf pro?"

"Yes, Roscoe Simms the golf pro. But it didn't last very long. You know how it is with the pro tour. He had to move on. I was so ashamed when he left."

"Don't worry, darling, the past is the past."

And that evening he made love beautifully to her, then rolled over to light a cigarette, and she said, "Roscoe wouldn't have done that."

"What?"

"Roscoe wouldn't have done that. He'd have made love to me all over again."

So he made love to her again, tenderly, caressing her to new heights. Afterward he got out of bed to relieve himself, and she said, "Roscoe wouldn't have done that."

"He wouldn't have?"

"No, he never stopped at only two."

He made love to her again, starting out tenderly and moving into a hard, grinding slam that had her clawing the bedspread. This time he made it to the bathroom and was feeling pretty good about his sexual prowess as he enjoyed the relief of urination. Her voice came from the room, "Roscoe wouldn't have stopped after three."

He came back into the room and picked up the phone.

"You calling room service?"

"No, I'm calling Roscoe. I want to find out what's par for this hole!"

Handcuffs

Grandpa Sloane had never taken a train ride in his life, and here he was bouncing and jostling along on a much ill-used, outmoded old coal-burner. Across from Grandpa Sloane sat two men joined by a pair of handcuffs. One was the deputy sheriff, and the other a furtive-eyed, shabby lout.

"Pardon me for askin', Depity," said Grandpa Sloane, "but why you got that man there in handcuffs?"

"Bugs," said the deputy sheriff.

"Come again?" said Grandpa Sloane.

"Nuts," said the shabby lout.

"Shame on you, Depity," chided Grandpa Sloane. "Keepin' a man in handcuffs with bugs on his nuts!"

Say Cheese!

"Darling, I'm going to be on the road again for three whole weeks," said Jim. "Three weeks is an awful long time when I love you as much as I do. You just don't know how much I miss you."

"Oh, Jim, honey, I miss you, too."

"But, darling, it's different for a man. I get so darn worked up thinking about you way back here and me way out there. If only I had a picture of your cunt to keep me company."

"Jim!"

"I know it sounds crazy, baby, but please let me take one of those instant pictures of your cunt."

"Jim! Whatever for?"

"Well, if I could take a peek at your sweet little fern whenever I get the urge, it would sure help me be true blue and loyal to you."

"If I let you take a picture of mine, could I take a picture of yours?"

"Wild Willie? Why would you want a picture of Wild Willie?"

"Well, while you're gone those three weeks, I could always take it in and have it enlarged!"

Nursery School

Pattie, Barbie, Donna, and Elaine were making sand-castles in the sandbox at nursery school when Pattie said, "My daddy's the greatest daddy in the whole world 'cause he can blow smoke out of his mouth."

"Oh, yeah?" challenged Donna. "My daddy's better than your daddy 'cause he can blow smoke out of his nose. I saw him do it. Yes, I did."

"Well," said Barbie, puffing up with self-impor-tance, "my daddy can blow smoke out of his ears!"

That little piece of information caused a round of little-girl giggling, which Elaine managed to break through by piping up with, "That's nothing. My daddy can blow smoke out of his asshole!"

The naughty word turned the giggling into hyster-ics, until Pattie could finally say, "Cannot."

"Can too!" said Elaine.

"You said a bad word," giggled Barbie.

"Cannot!" insisted Pattie.

"I said he can do it, and I know he can!" shouted Elaine.

"How do you know that?" asked Donna.

"Because," answered Elaine.

"Because why?" demanded Pattie.

"Because I saw the nicotine stains in his under-pants, that's why!" screamed Elaine.

A Proper English Wedding

Chief Bwanabangi of Tanzaswazi in central Africa wanted a very proper English wedding for the youngest daughter of his favorite wife. From a faded and much-creased newspaper clipping of an English newspaper's society page, he had the entire wedding ceremony re-created, right down to the flower arrangements, top hats, morning coats, and the bride's gown. The only thing not very proper English was the shoes. He just couldn't get his people to wear shoes.

The June wedding was held on a spectacular African day, and it went off without a hitch . . . almost. When the bridegroom was to slip the ring on the bride's finger, he dropped it, and it rolled out of his easy reach. As the hapless bridegroom scrambled to retrieve the errant ring, an ancient, naked elder darted into the gathering and at random pinched several ladies' breasts, then darted out when the ring had been retrieved.

That evening as Chief Bwanabangi was being praised, a jealous rival chief challenged the role of the naked elder in a truly proper English wedding. Chief Bwanabangi was outraged and pulled out his faded newspaper clipping.

"You see!" he bellowed. "It says right here, 'When the bridegroom dropped the ring, a nervous titter ran through the crowd!' "

Rub-a-Dub-Dub

Rub-a-dub-dub, three men in a tub—the senator, the governor, the Supreme Court justice—didn't see sub. Glub glub.

It had been the largest gathering of administration officials with their wives and children in the history of the country. When the president was reelected for an unprecedented fifth term, the luxury liner *QE 2* was put at his disposal for the grandest inaugural bash ever.

The press coverage was worldwide, and the *QE 2* a sitting duck for the enemy's new, secret stealth submarine. She took sixteen high-powered torpedoes before an alarm was even raised. The once-reigning queen of the sea was sinking faster than a turd in a punch bowl. The senator, the governor, and the Supreme Court justice found themselves together on an upper deck.

"My God! We're sinking!" screamed the governor wildly. "Save the women and children!"

"Ah, fuck 'em!" shouted the Supreme Court justice.

"Certainly," said the senator, checking his watch. "But do we have the time?"

He and She

"Do you know why women have cunts?" he asked.
  "No, why?"
"So men will talk to them!"
"Do you know why men have balls?" she asked.
"No, why?"
"Because they don't have brains!"
"What is a woman?" he asked.
"What?"
"A life-support system for a vagina!"
"What's long and hard for a man?" she asked.
"What?"
"Third grade!"
"Why do women have legs?" he asked.
"Why?"
"So they won't leave snail trails when they walk!"
"What's ten and a half inches on a man?" she asked.
"What?"
"Nothing!"
"What did the blind man say when he passed the
fish market?" he asked.
  "What?"
"Afternoon, ladies!"
"What's a pimple on a man's ass?" she asked.
"What?"
"A brain tumor!"

"Can you imagine what fish would taste like if women didn't swim?" he asked.

"Do you like apples?" she asked.

"Yes."

"Good. Let's fuck!"

"My place or yours?"

"If you're going to talk about it all day, forget it!"

Hound Dog

Richard and Greg staggered out of the bar around three o'clock in the morning, arms draped around each other's shoulders for support.

"Hey, Richard," said Greg, "look at that old hound dog lying there by the curb licking his balls!"

"Huh?" said Richard, peering toward the dog like an owl with a glass eye. "Yeah, looks like he's having a real good time."

"You know why dogs lick their balls?" asked Greg.

"No," hiccuped Richard. "Why?"

"Because they can!" roared Greg with drunken laughter.

"Gee," said Richard, eyeballing the dog enviously. "Wish I could do that."

"You probably can," said Greg. "But you better pet him first!"

Don't Make a Wave

The bug-eyed demon of Hell spoke with a rasping, choked voice as it explained to Barry he'd have to choose between three closed doors, and the choice would determine how he would spend eternity in Satan's domain.

"And if you pass a door, but don't like the one you do choose, you can't go back," rasped the demon, smoke curling from its cracked lips.

Barry paused and listened at door number one. From within he heard the raucous sounds of a never-ending party.

"Quite tempting, but parties tend to be a bore, don't you think?" Barry asked the demon, who was busy tearing great gashes in its own flesh with its filthy claws.

"Yes, I see," said Barry and moved to door number two. He found the sounds of whips biting and screams of pain amusing, but hardly the way to spend eternity. After all, who was the whipper and who the whippee?

Barry pressed his ear to door number three, straining to hear a break in the silence. He'd never heard anything as silent as the silence coming from behind door number three. "I say, jolly-ho, sounds like a room needs a bit of livening up, eh?"

The demon chewed off three fingers, a thumb, and a large portion of its left hand as it fumbled for the key to door number three with the other. When door number three swung open the ruddiness drained from Barry's cheeks as he saw the endless expanse of liquid excrement dotted with human faces straining to keep their lips above the frothy stew of waste.

"Don't make a wave," said a weak voice off to his right.

"Ted? Is that you?"

"Don't make a wave!"

"My God, Ted, how can you stand this?" whined Barry as he slid gently into the warm stench.

"You ain't seen nothing yet, mate. Every afternoon around four, your wife tears through in Satan's speedboat!"

Propriety

"Oh, Mary darling, would you mind—"

"Don't call me Mary, and I'm not your darling!"

"What?"

"You heard me. Don't call me Mary. I only allow my closest and most intimate friends to call me by my first name. It's Miss Delgado to you."

"Well, excuse me all to Hell and back, Miss Delgado."

"That's better."

"Now, Miss Delgado, would you mind moving your ass over to the left a little bit. One of my nuts is getting crushed."

Thou Shalt Not Want

"My God," said the shepherd as he and his flock broke into the meadow clearing, "how lovely!" Before him stretched a small field of buttercups, glowing delicately golden in the summer afternoon light.

"Look, Pinky," he said to his favorite ewe, "aren't they lovely!" Pinky bleated her assent, farted, and began to munch his shirttail.

With a profound respect for natural beauty, particularly Pinky's, the shepherd herded his flock around the meadow so not one buttercup would be crushed. After two hours they were all safely around, and the shepherd paused to look back at the golden loveliness one last time before plodding on to the high meadow.

"Shepherd," rumbled a deep voice from nowhere in particular and everywhere at once.

"Yes, Lord," said the shepherd, not doubting for an instant the origination of that voice.

"Shepherd, thou hast pleased Me very much for sparing this field of humble buttercups. No matter where thou art or what thou endeavor from this moment forward, thou shalt not want for butter."

"Butter? Well, thank you very much, Lord. But where the Hell were you a couple of months ago when I circled that patch of pussy willows?!"

Chee-Chee!

Two Presbyterian missionaries were captured by a savage African tribe. They were trussed up like two pigs bound for market and dragged before the chief.

"Make choice," intoned the chief. "Death or *chee-chee!*"

The older missionary began to weep, and to set a good example, the young missionary squared his shoulders as much as the bindings allowed and said in a loud voice, "In the name of Jesus Christ, *chee-chee!*"

The tribal warriors yelped their delight, unbound the young missionary, stripped him naked, bent him over a log, and tied him in that unfortunate position. Then, drunk and lusty on the local brew, they all buggered him into unconsciousness.

Seeing his young friend hanging limply over the log, broken and bleeding, the older missionary gathered his courage and looked the chief straight in the eye when the chief said, "Make choice. Death or *chee-chee!*"

"Death!" answered the older missionary.

"Good choice," said the chief wisely. Then with a wicked grin, he added, "But first, *chee-chee!*"

Dirty Dave and the Clocks of Hell

One of Hell's attendants was showing a new arrival around the premises when the new arrival said, "I can't help noticing the vast number of pendulum clocks everywhere I look. But none of them seems to be keeping the right time. Some aren't even running, some are running, some are running much too slowly, and some too fast. What's it mean?"

"These clocks aren't for keeping time; they're for keeping track."

"Keeping track of what?" asked the new arrival.

"You see the little name tag on the bottom of each clock? There's a clock here for every man alive today. They only run when their living counterparts are jerking off. Some don't run very often, some run slow, some run fast. Get it?"

"Yes, I get it. But I haven't noticed a clock with my old buddy Dirty Dave's name on it."

"Oh, that one. Yeah, I got a clock for *that one*. Keep it in my office. Use it as a fan!"